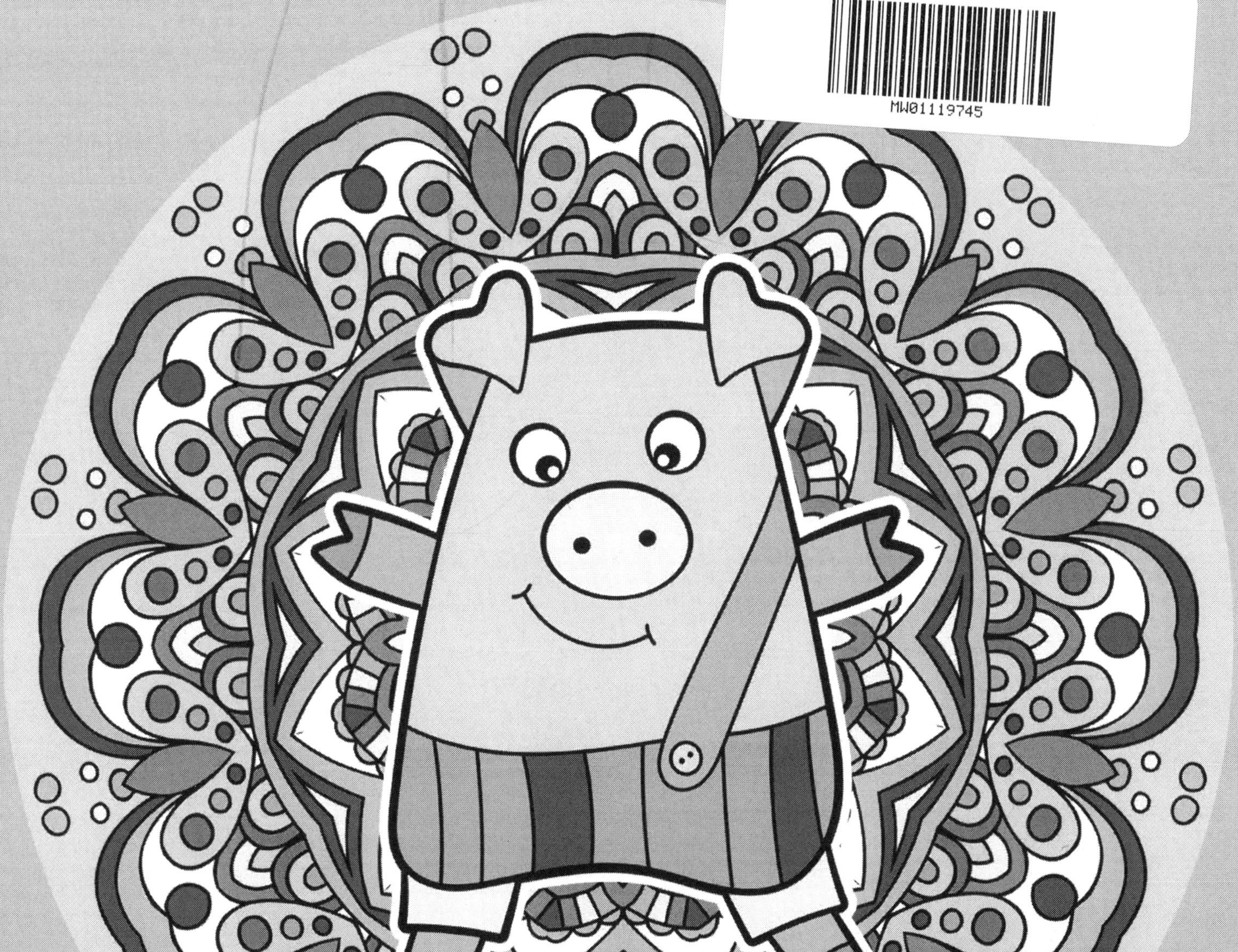

PIGDALAS

COLORING BOOKS

Doodle Art Designs for Relaxation and Mindfulness

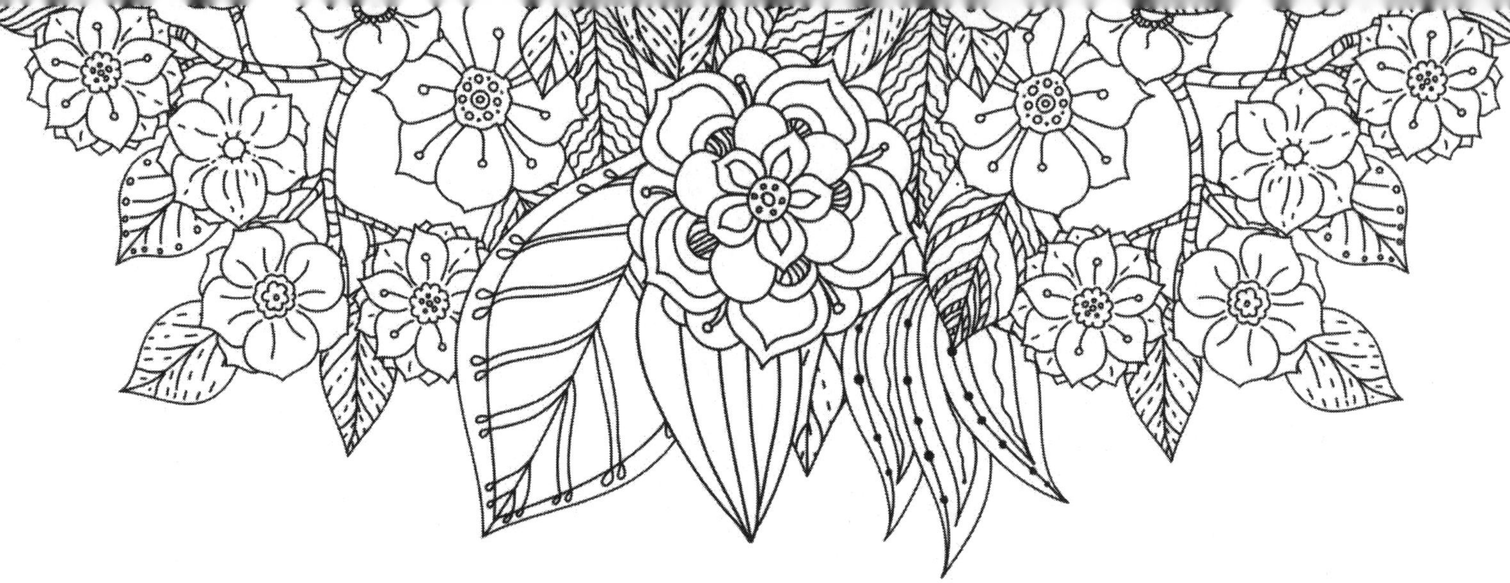

UNICORN COLORING

Printed in U.S.A.

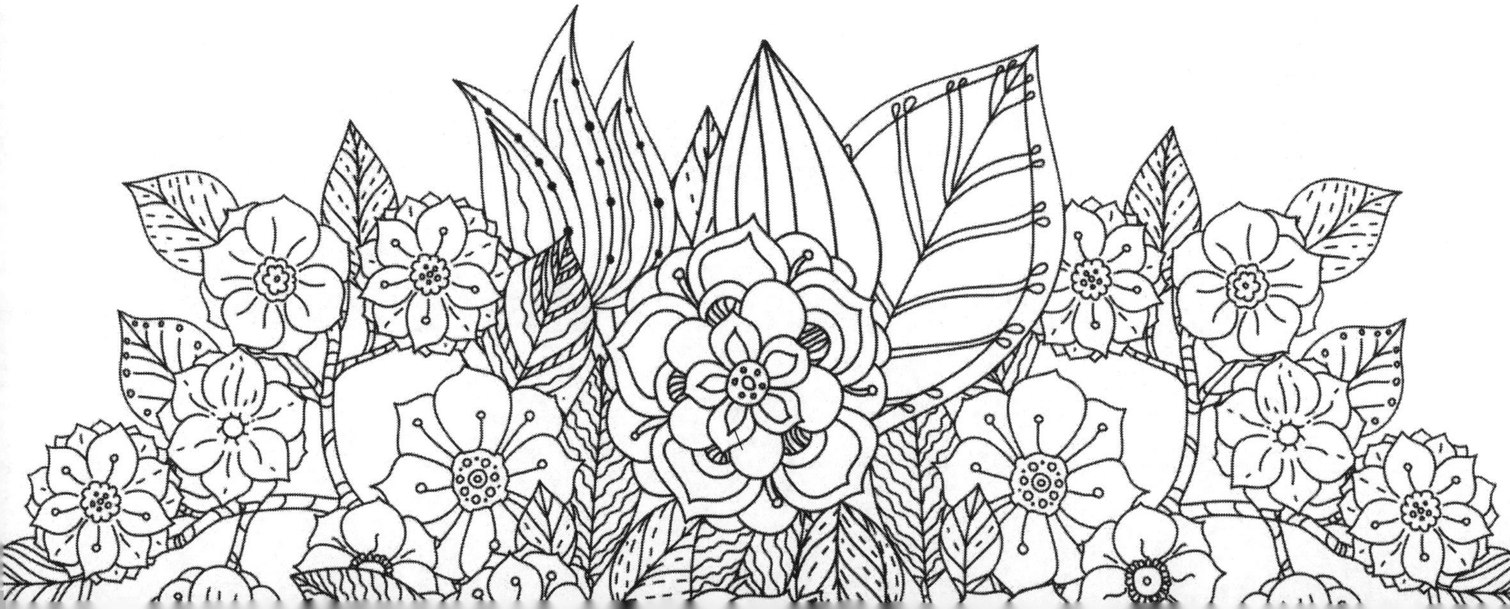

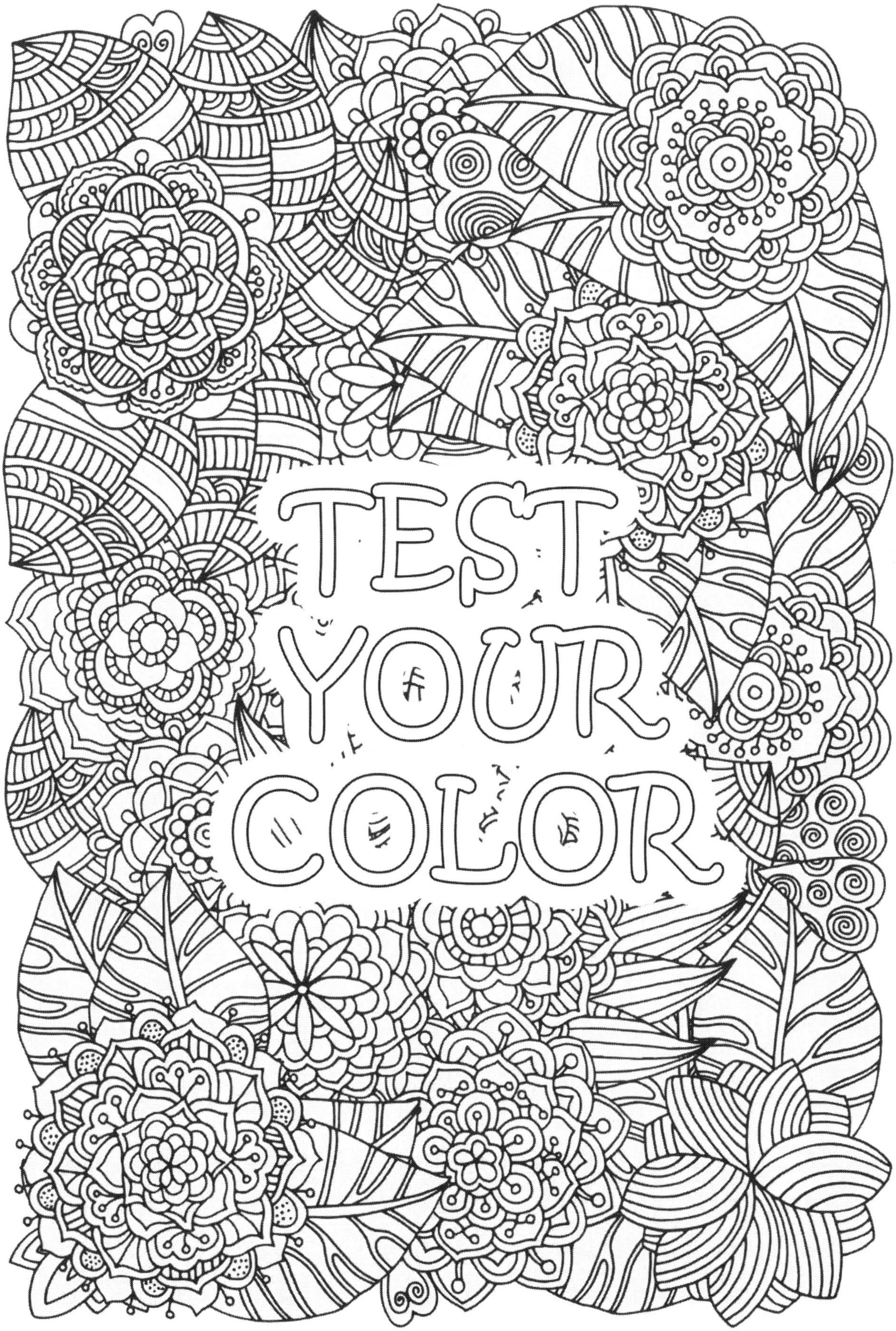
TEST
YOUR
COLOR

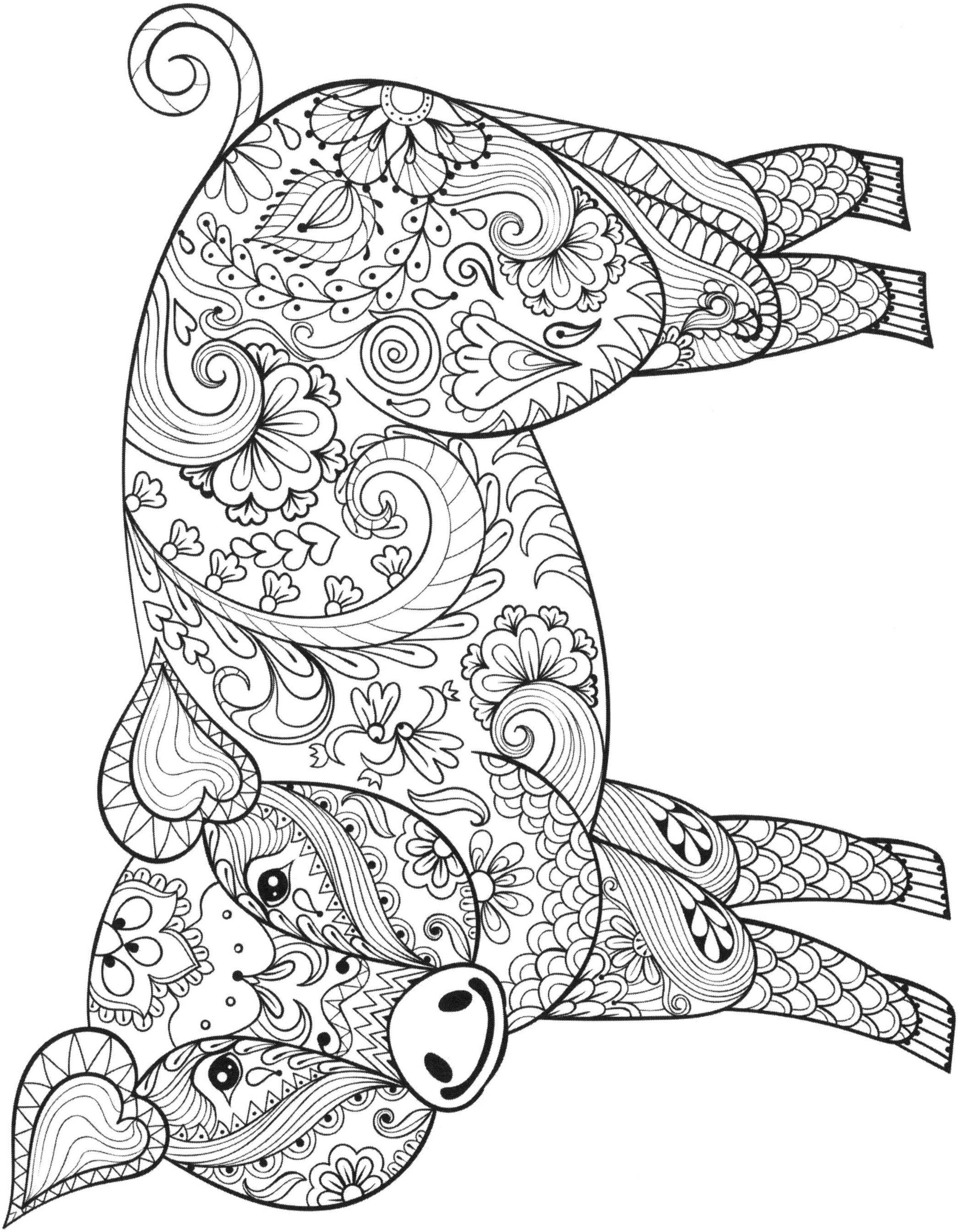

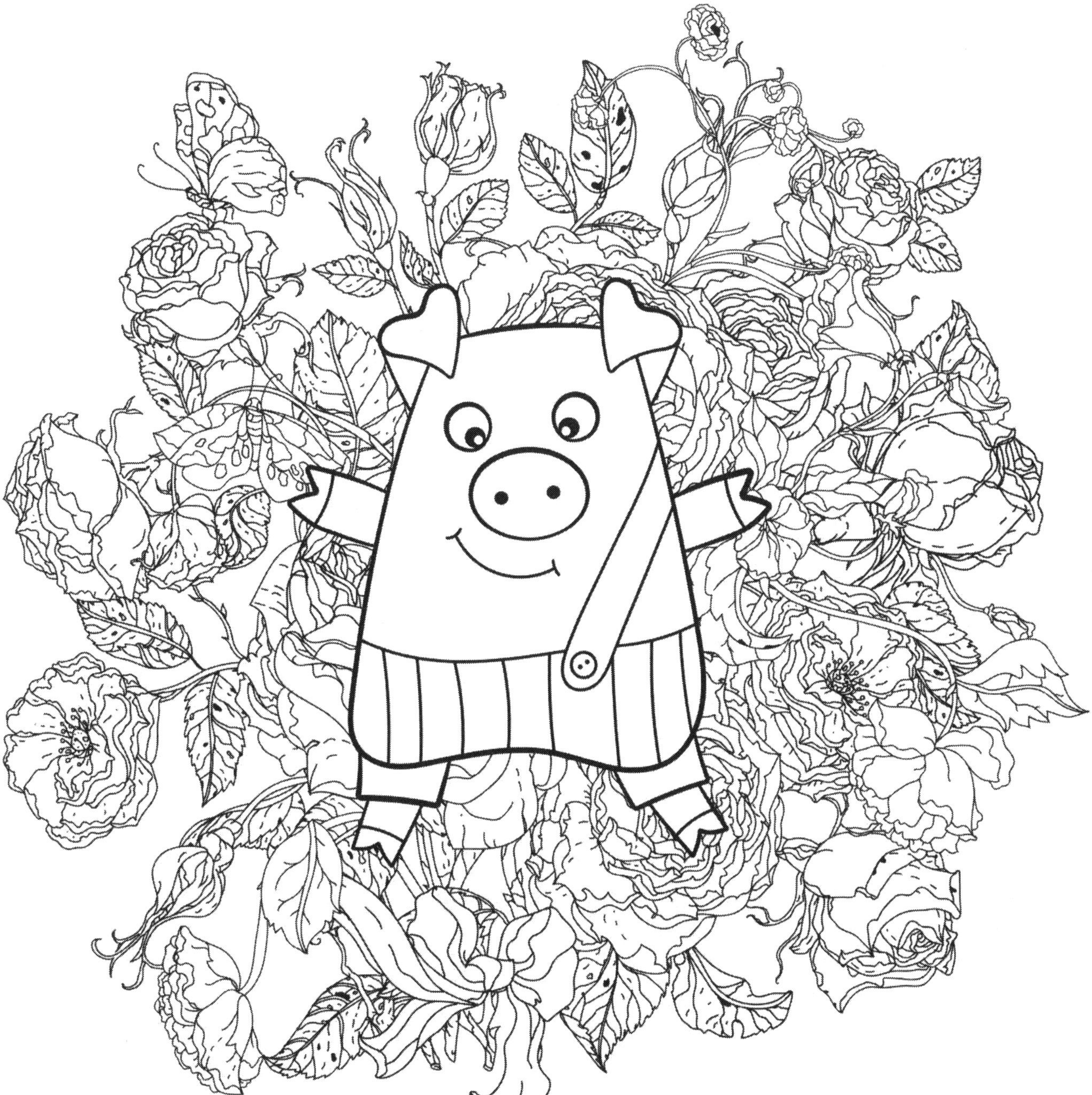

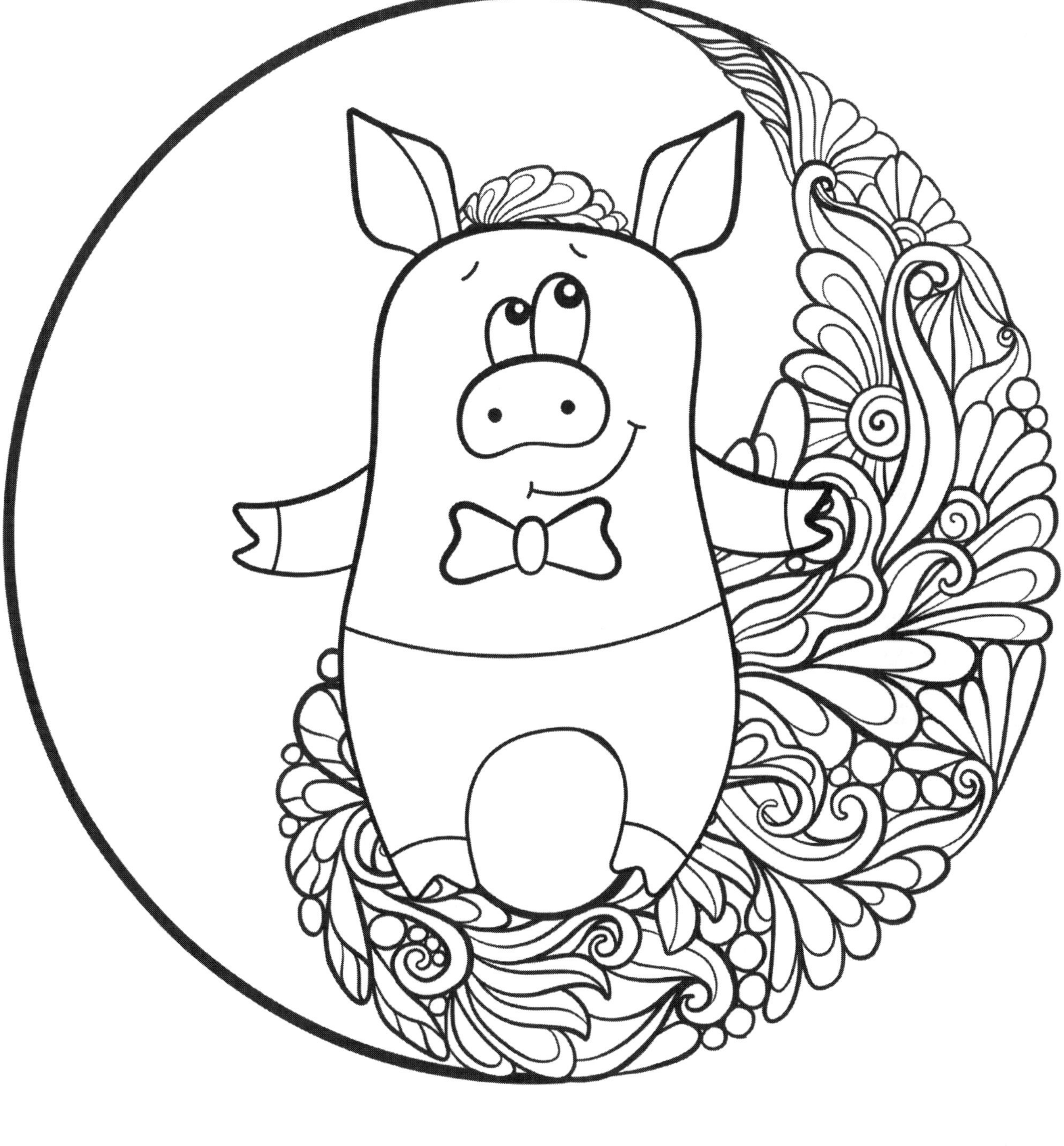

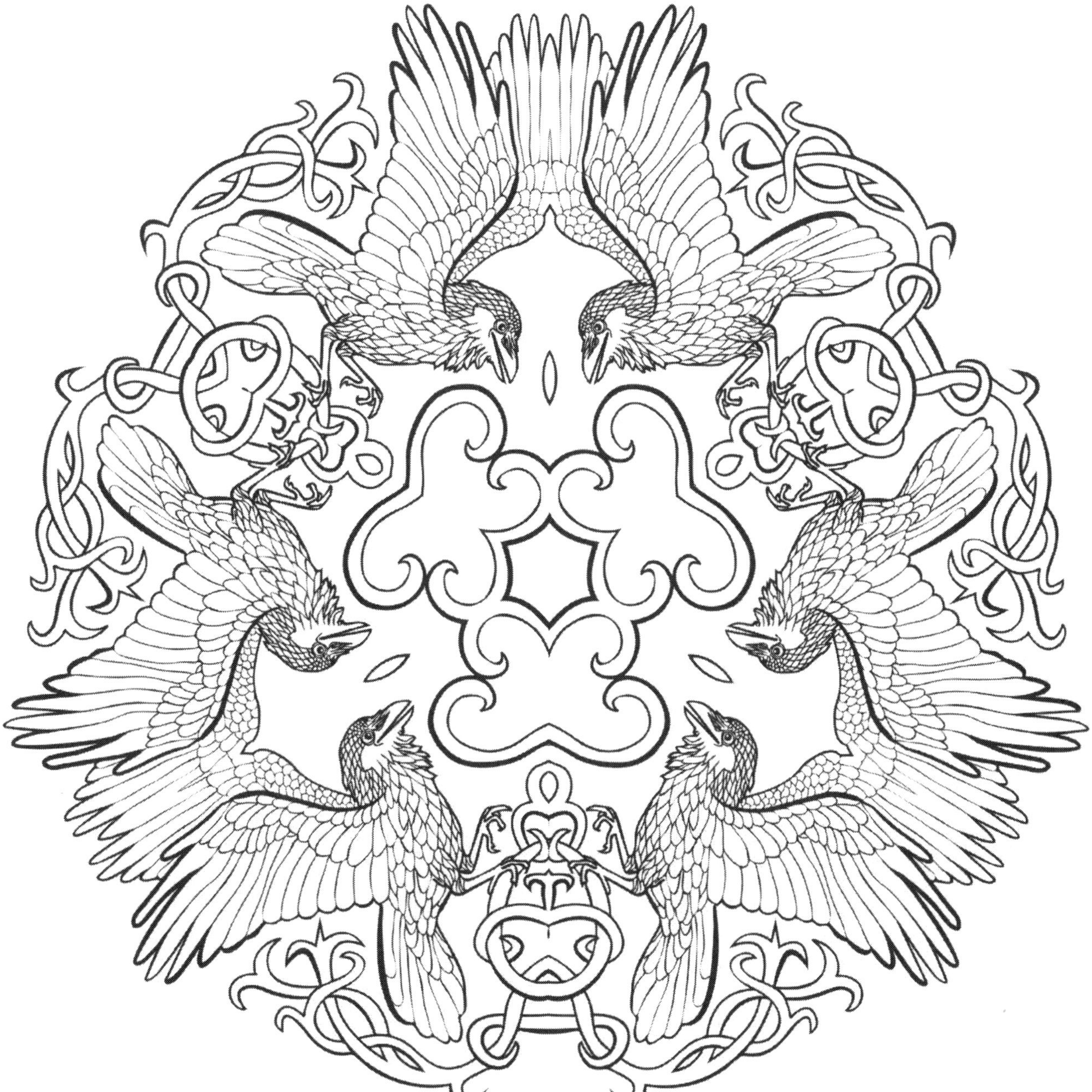

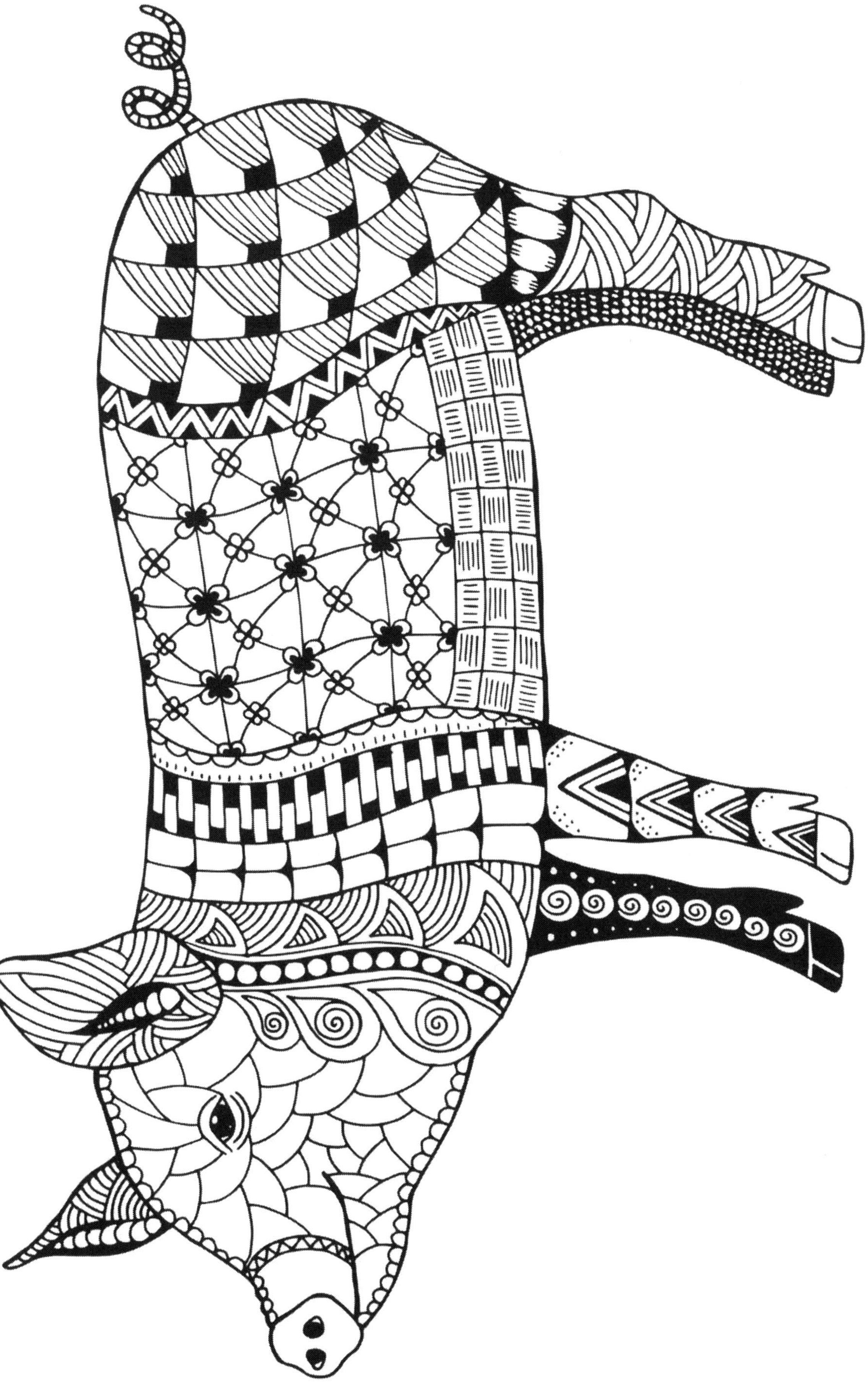

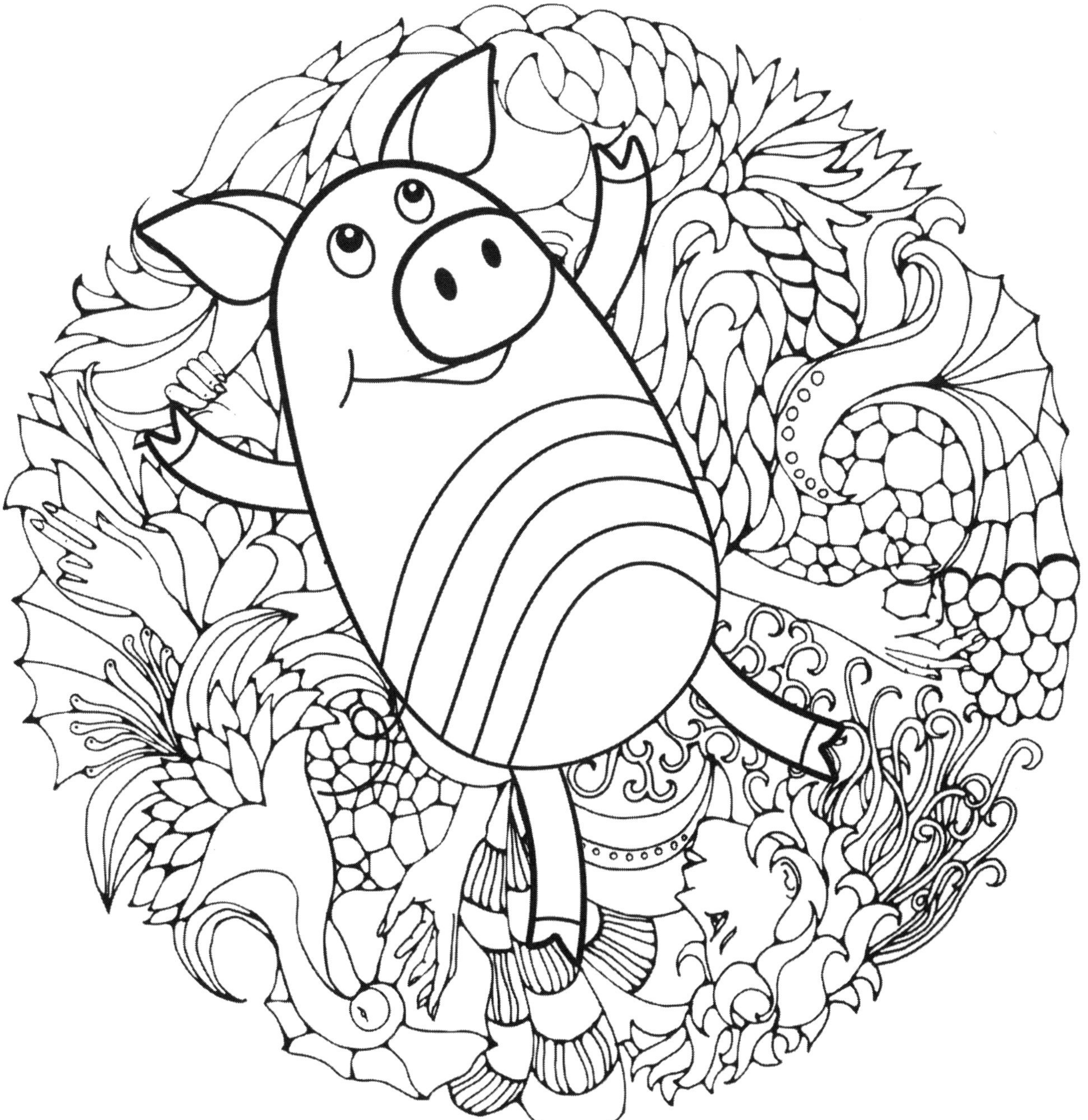

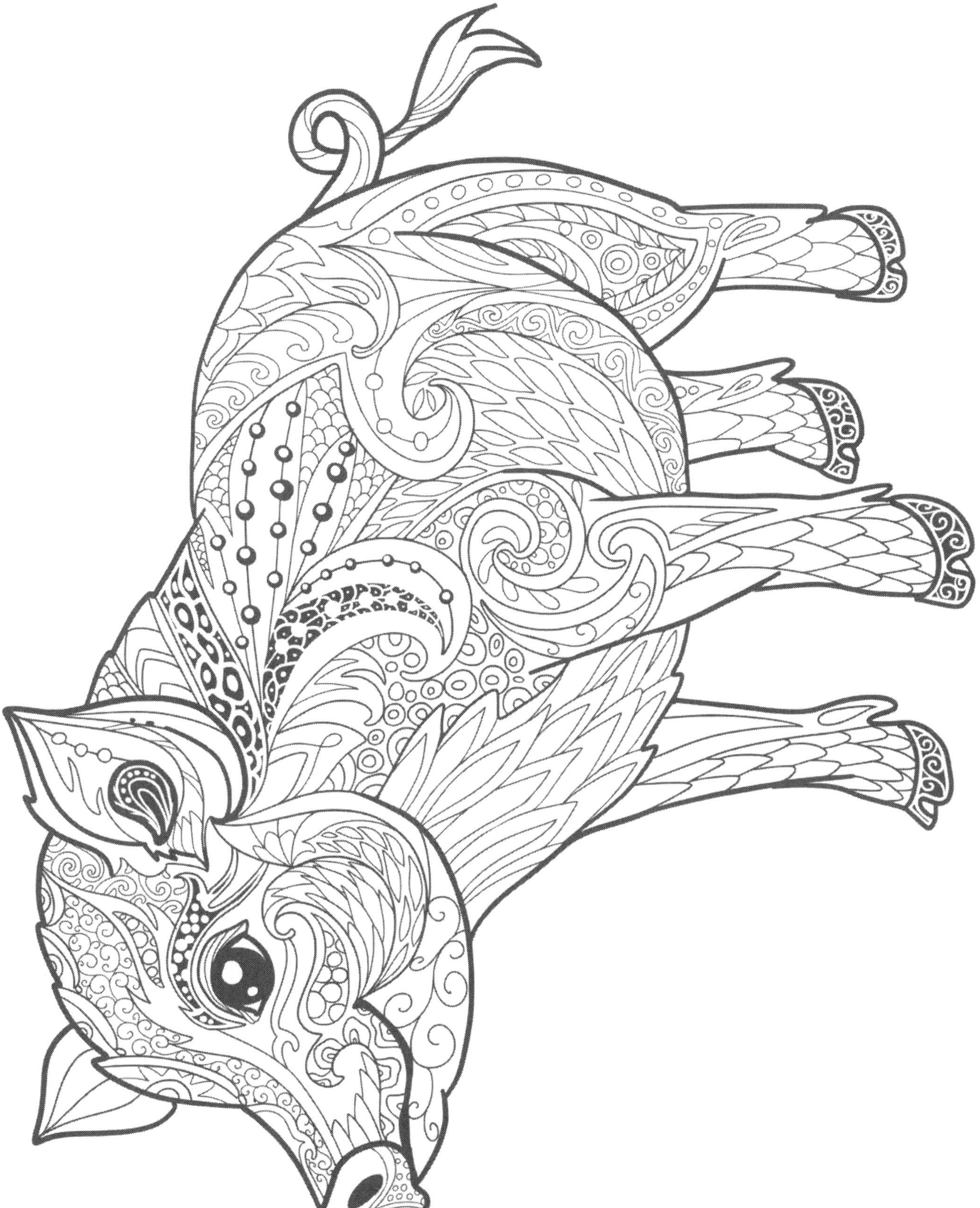

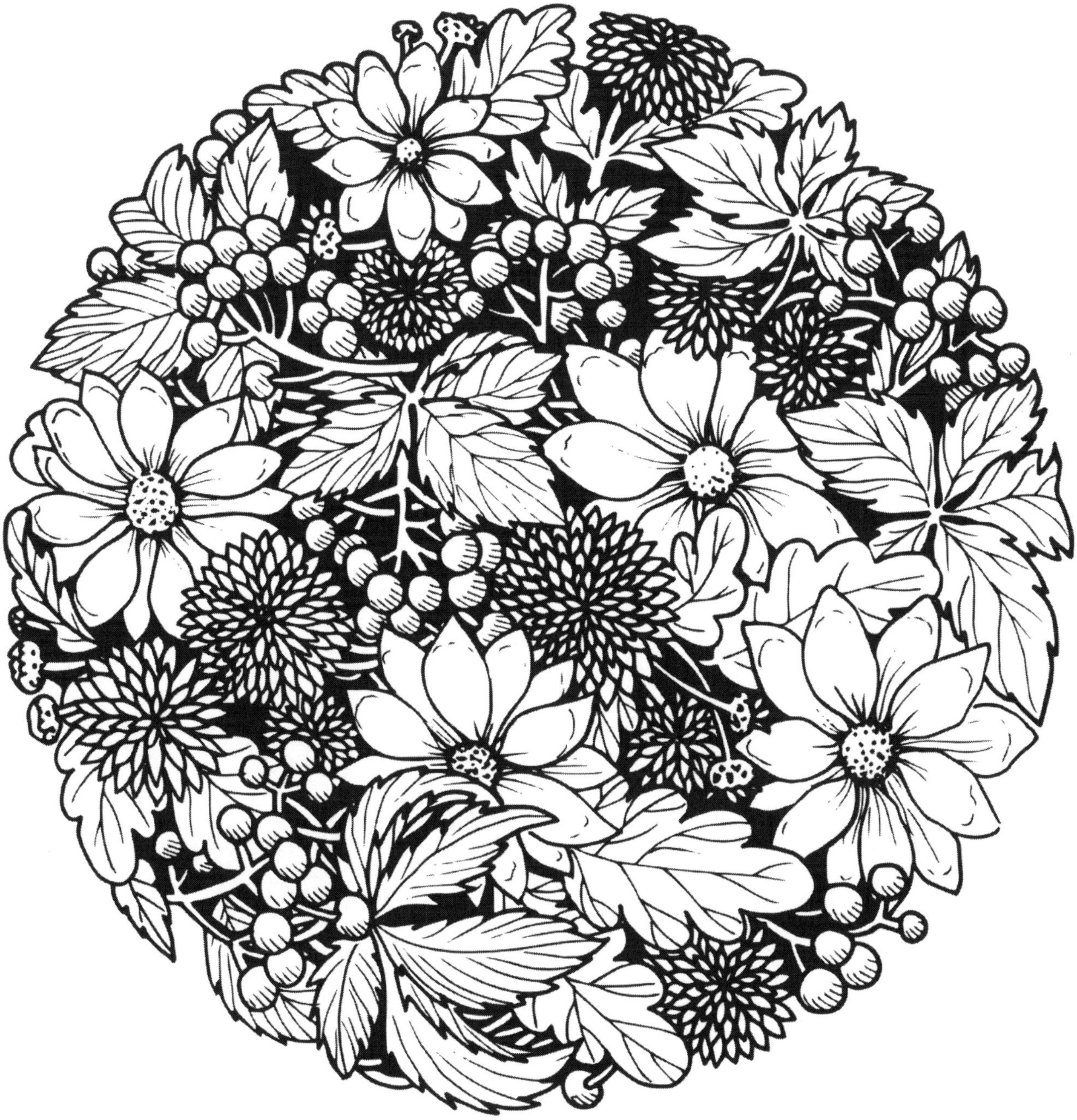

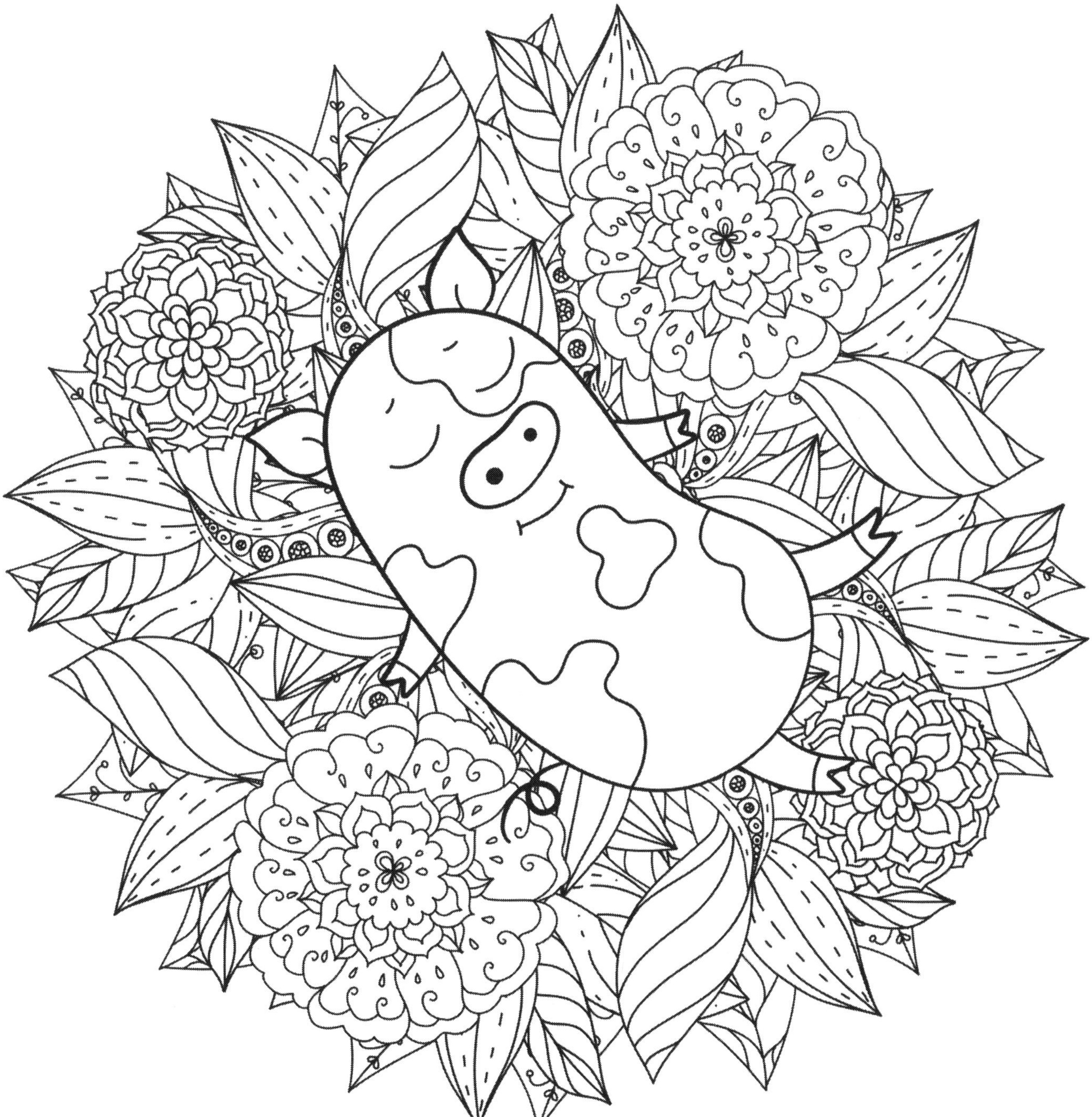

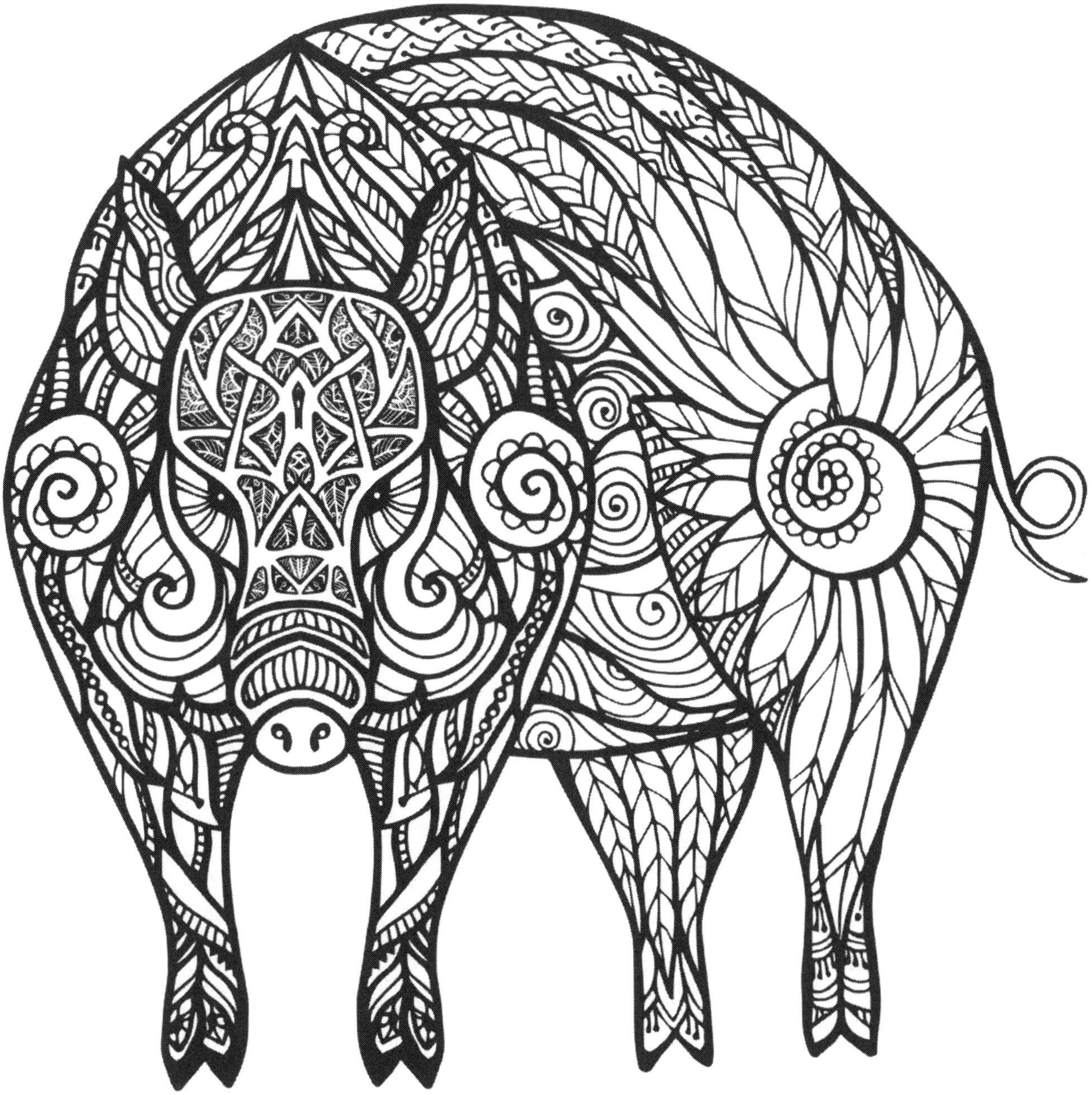

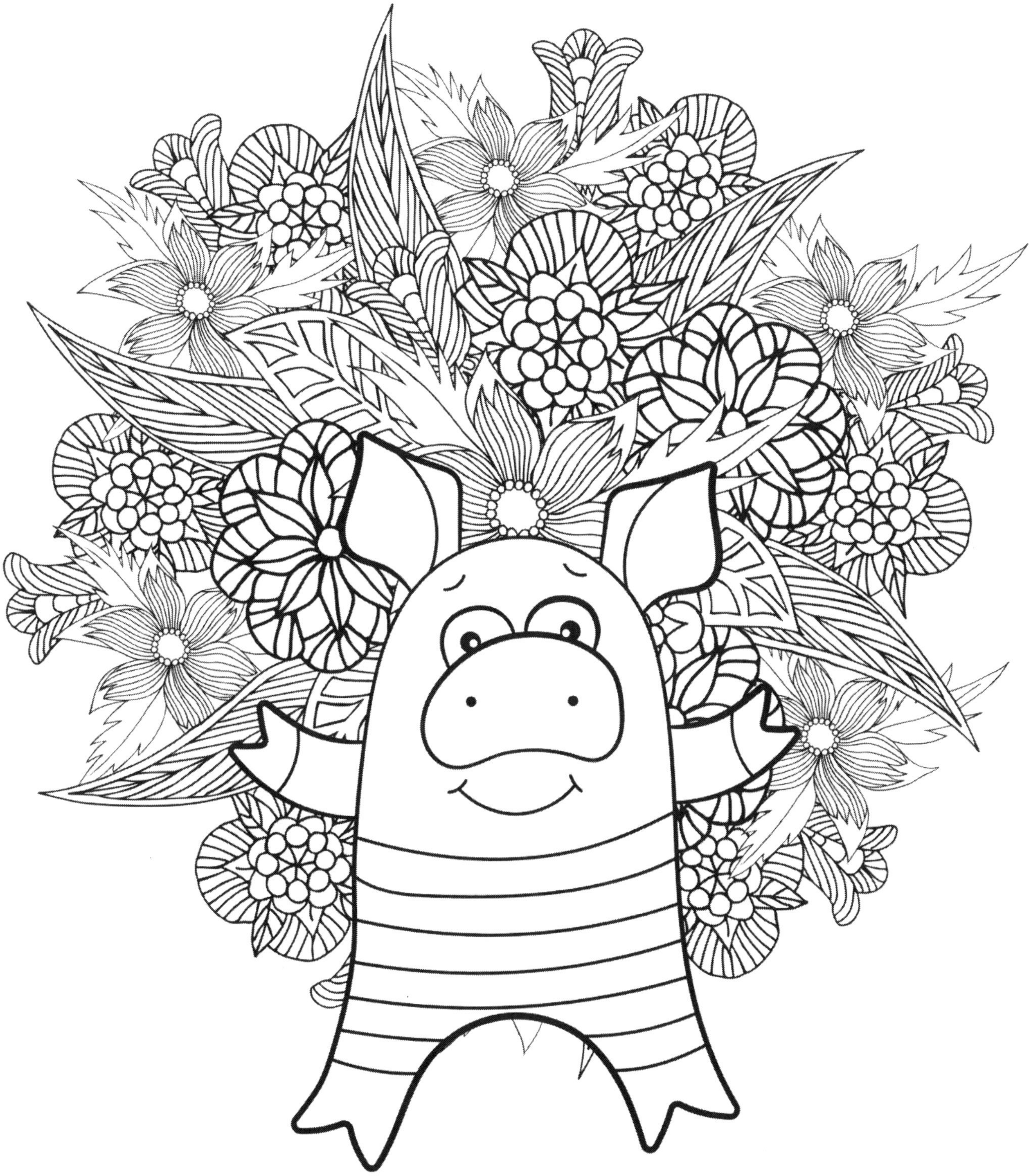

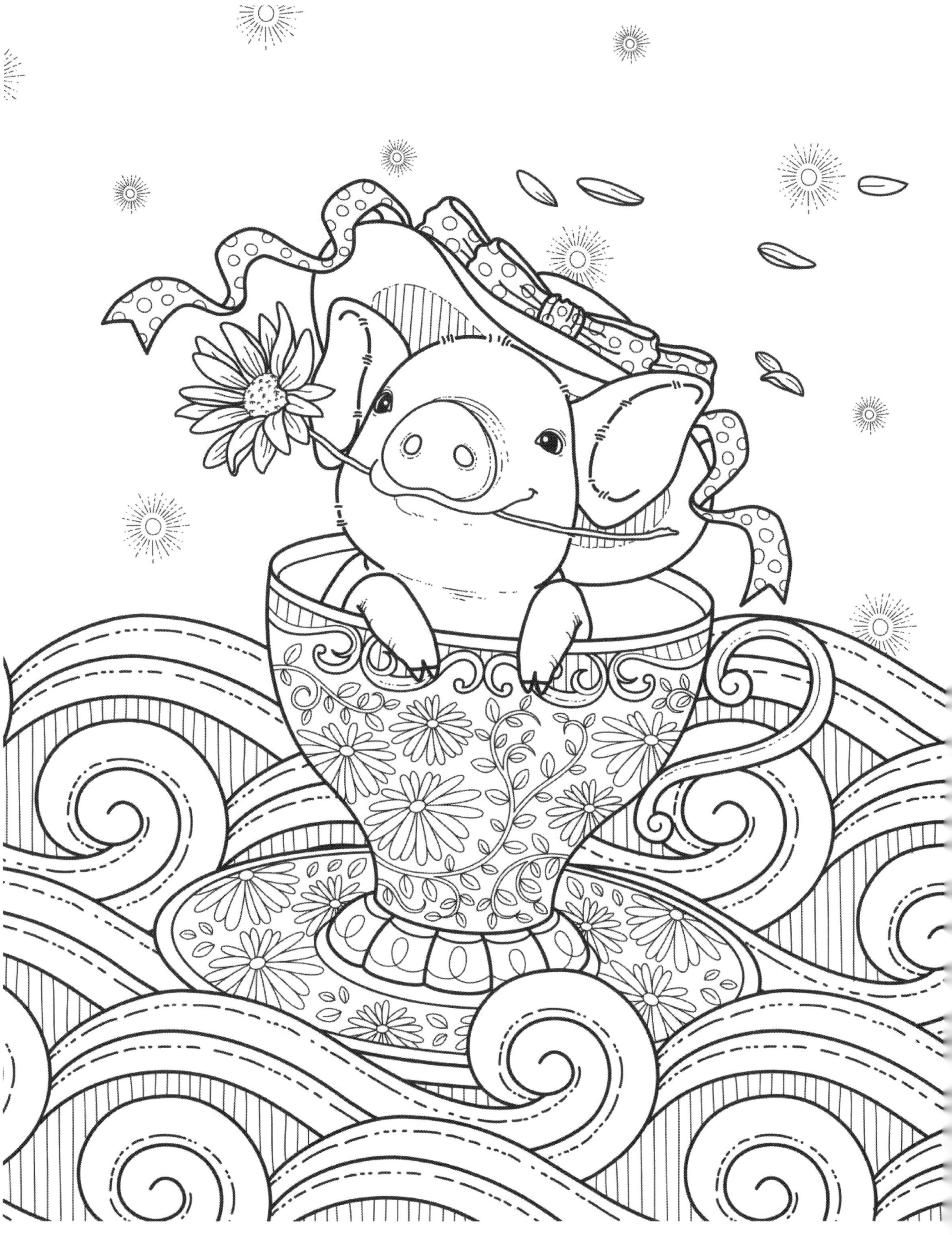

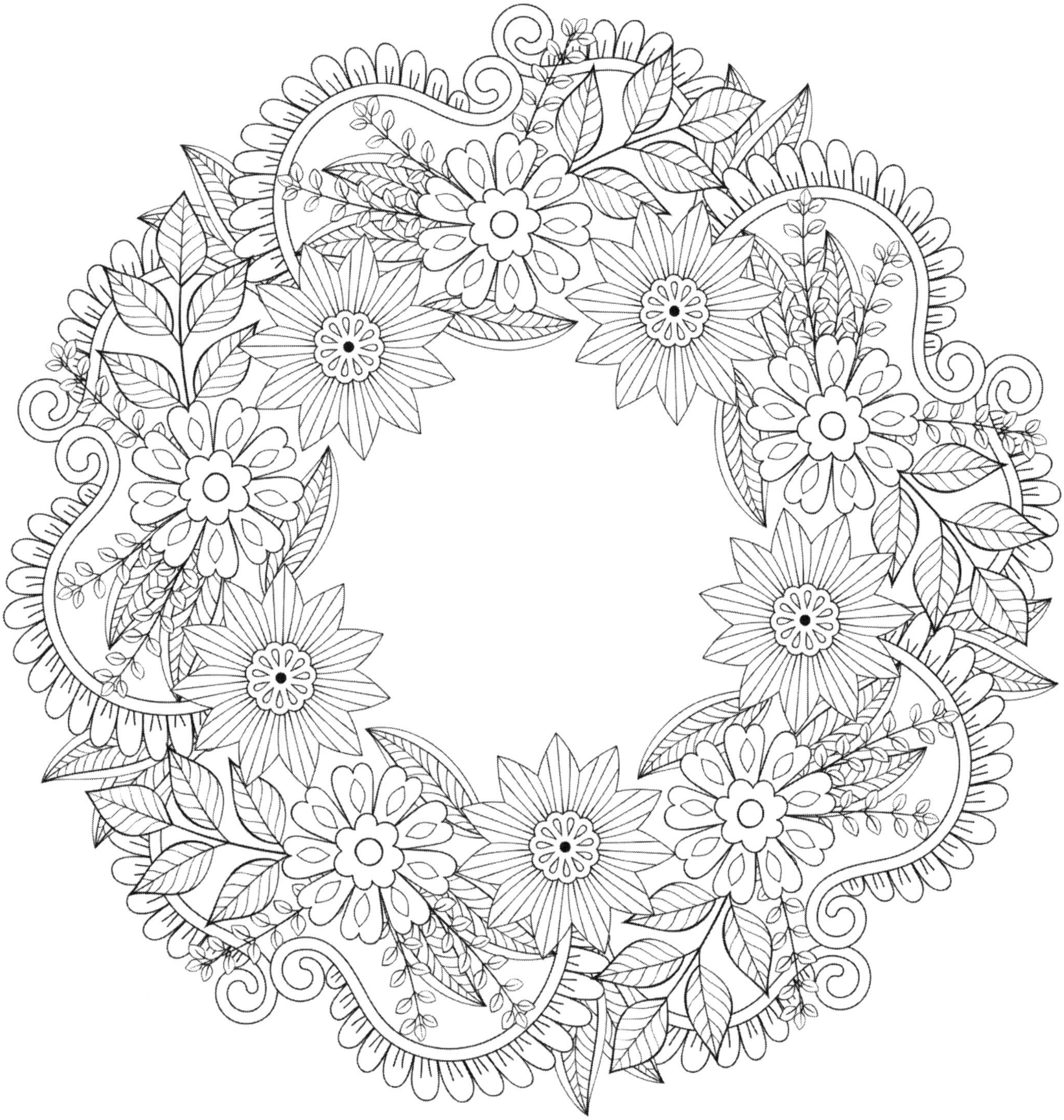

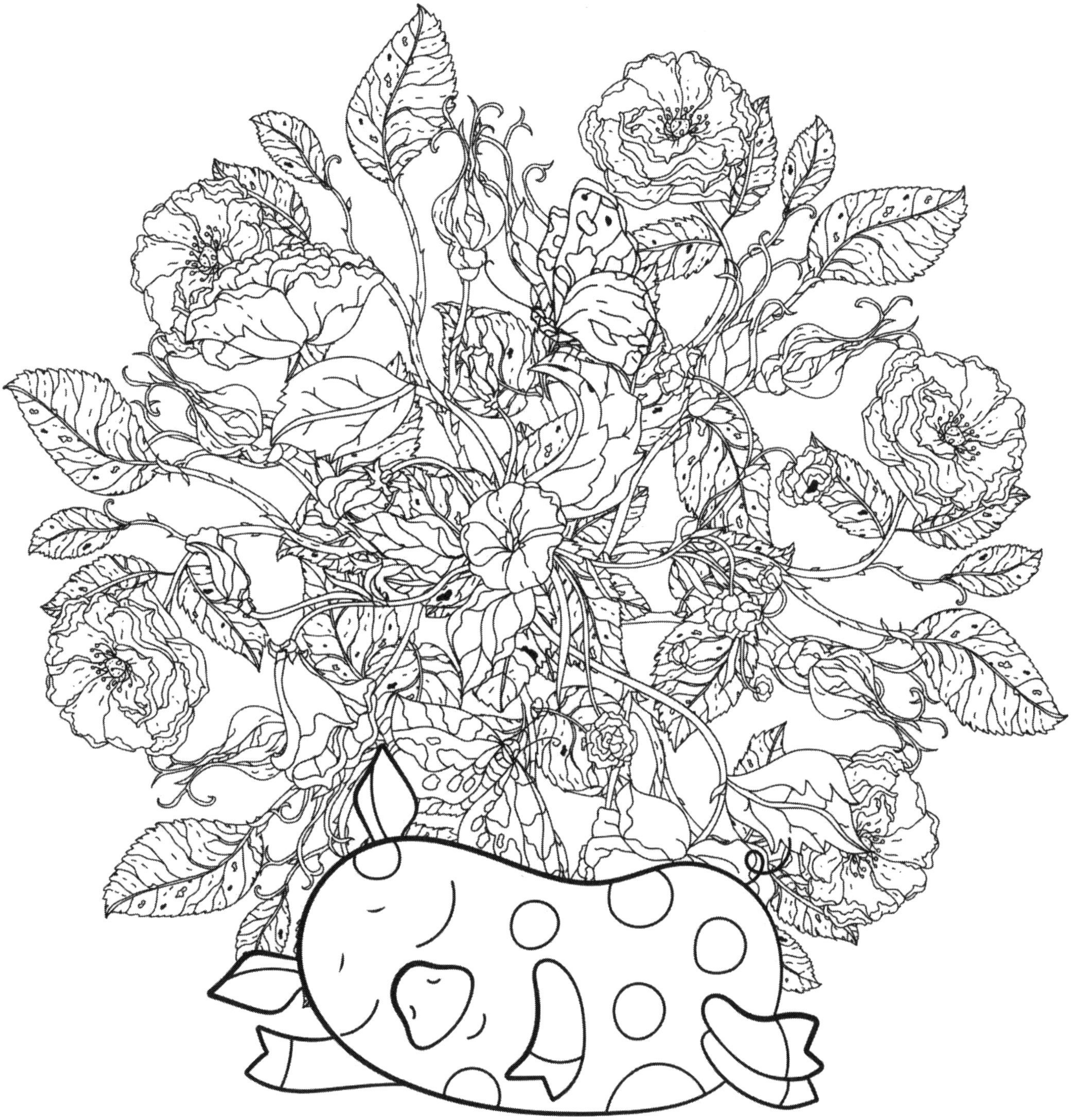

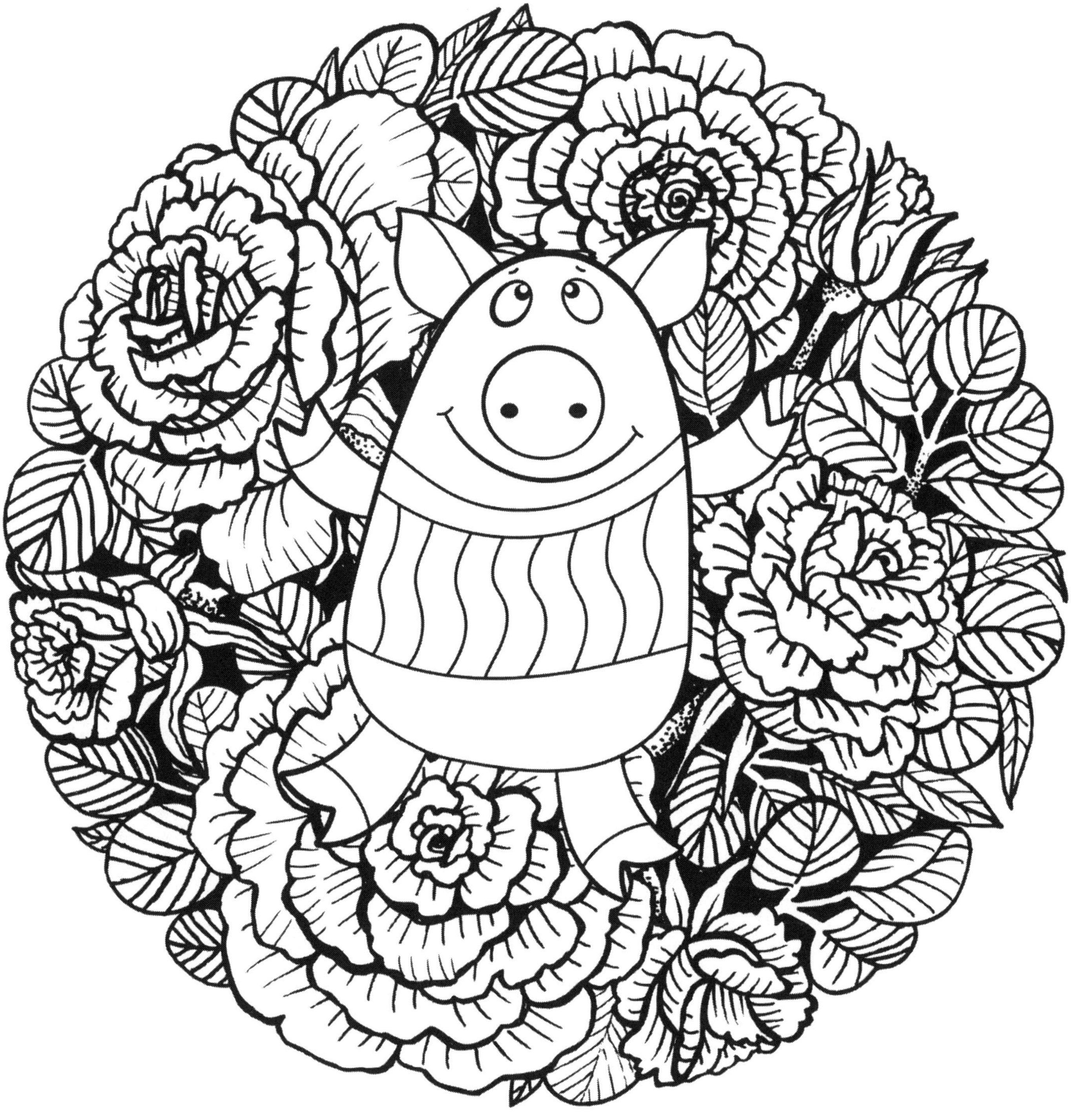

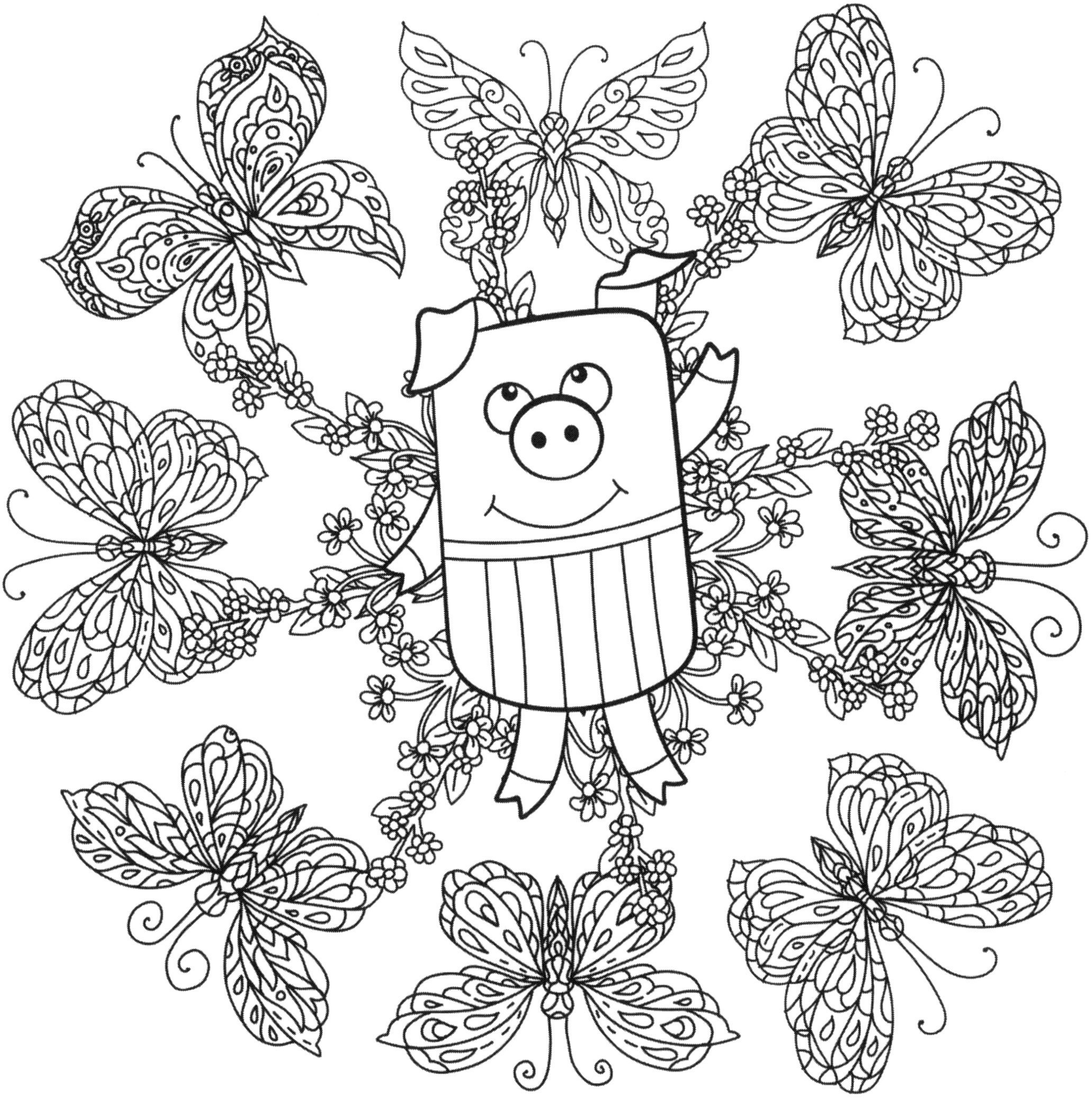

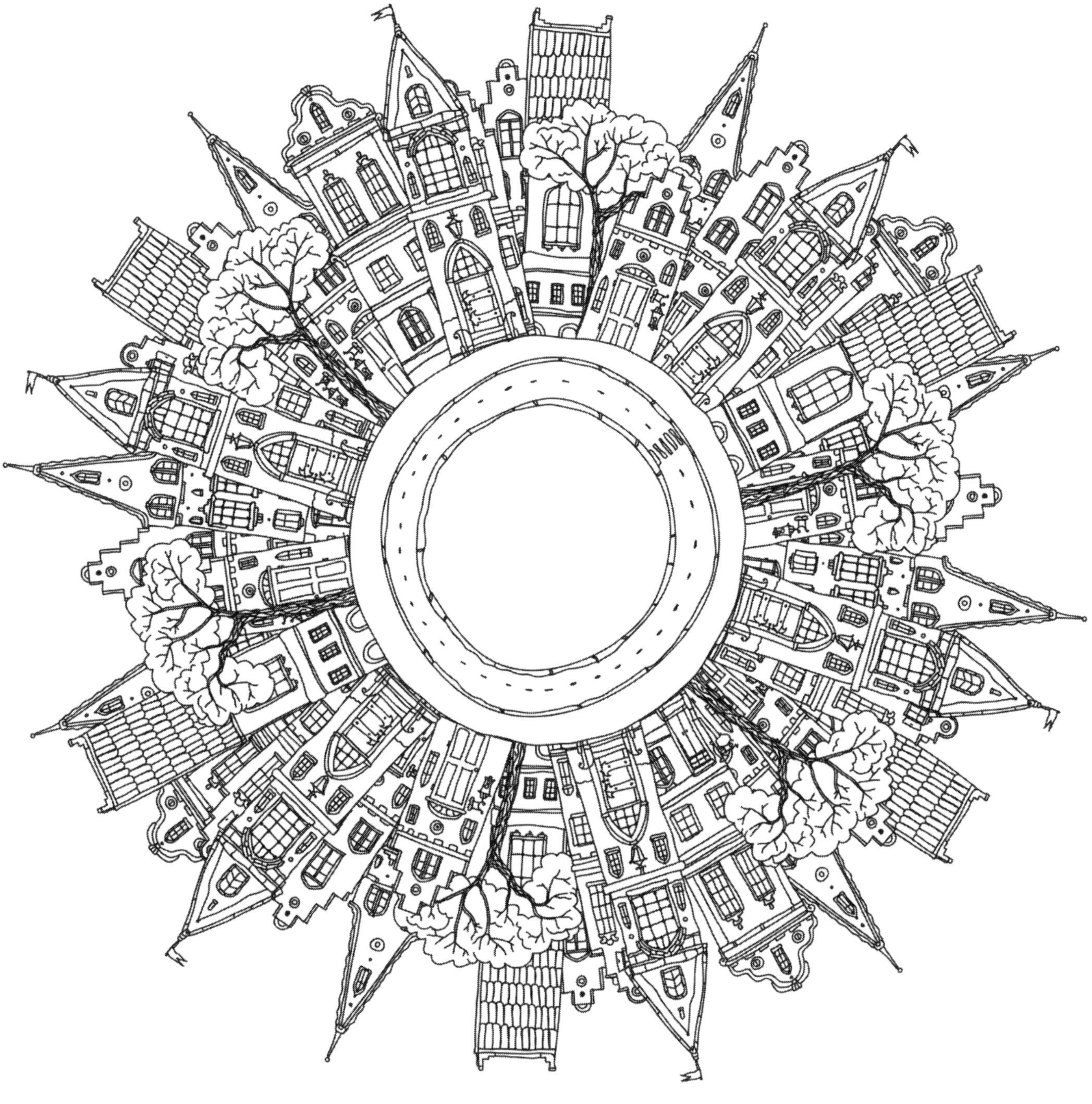

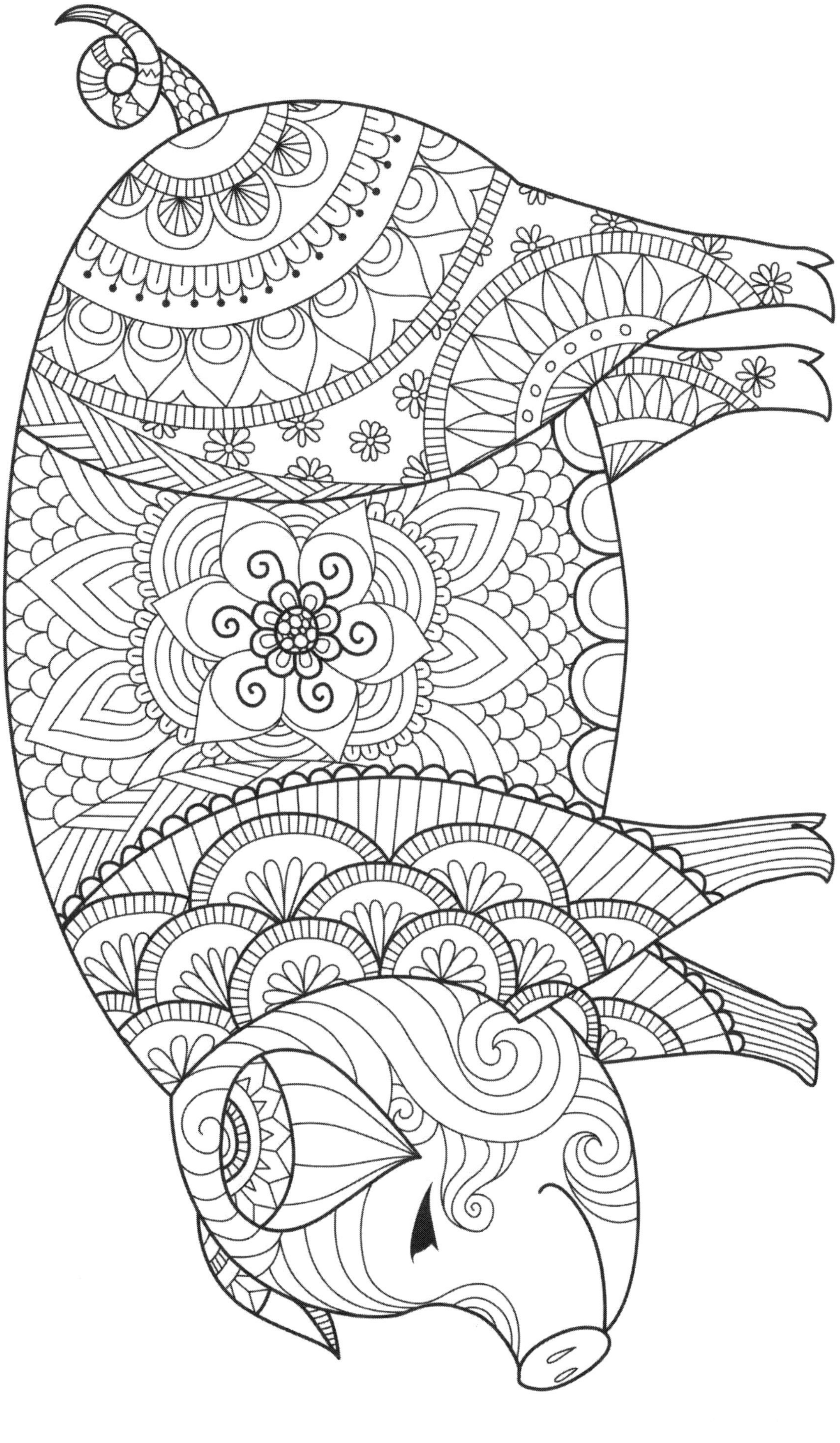

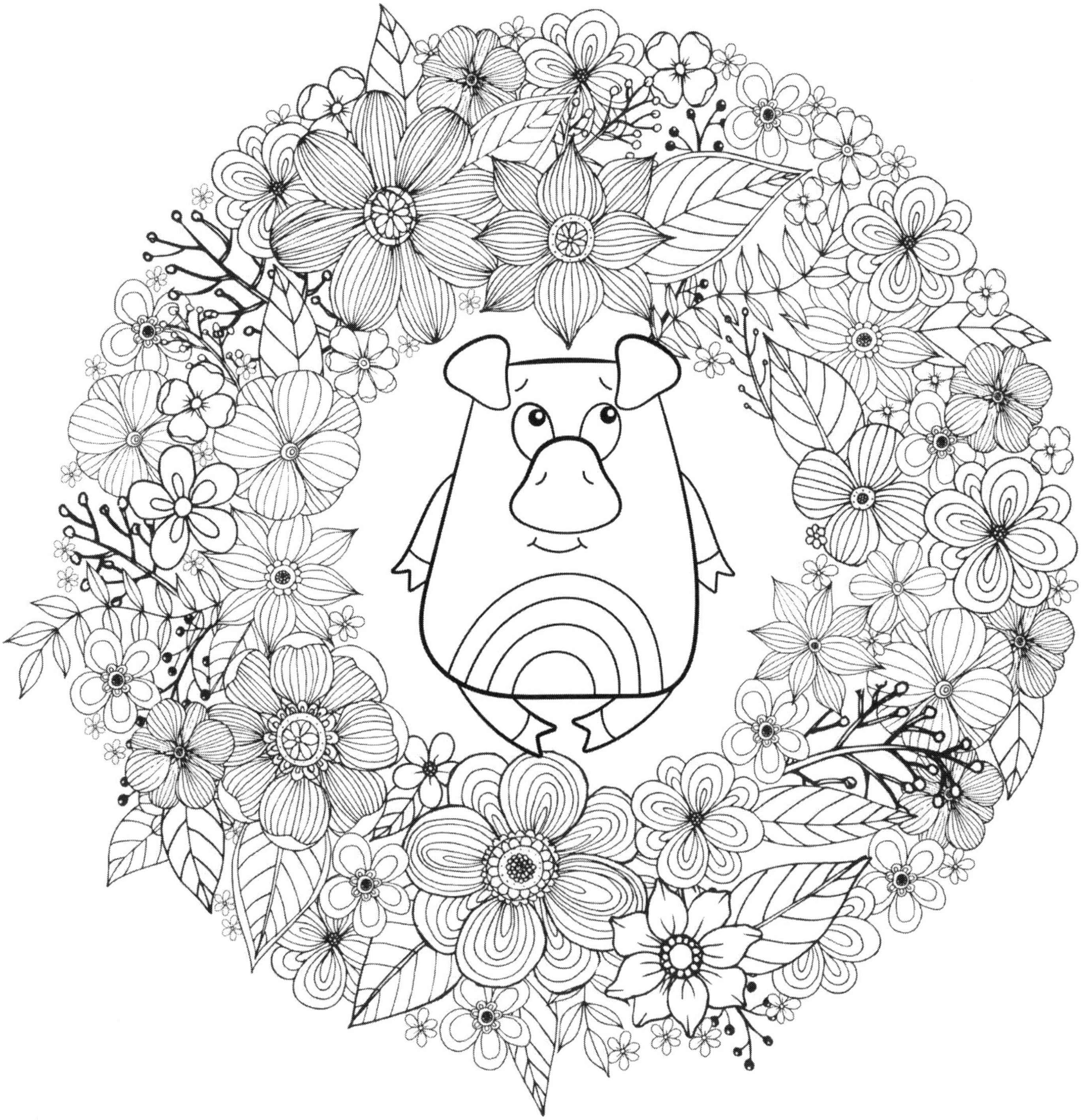

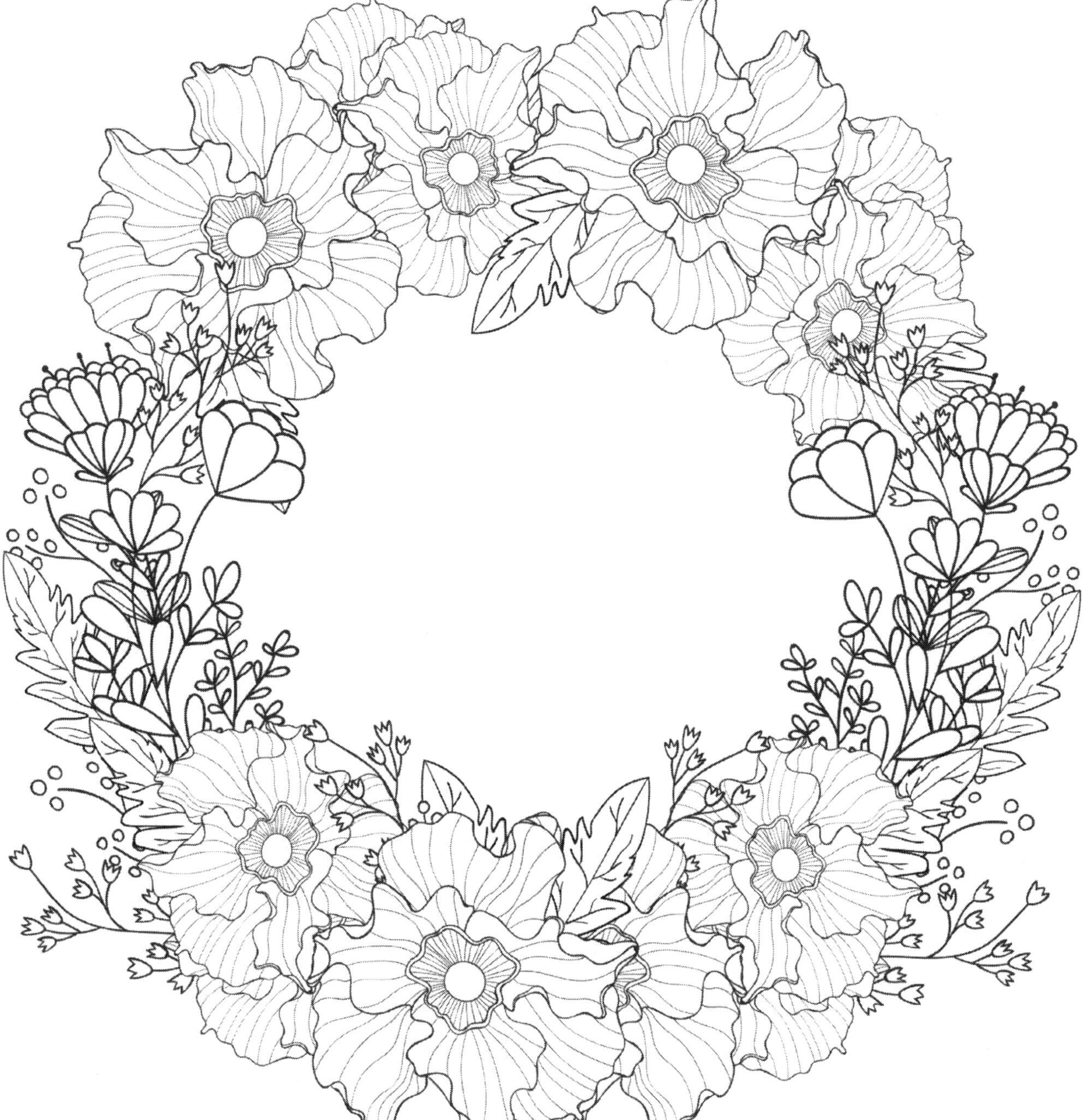

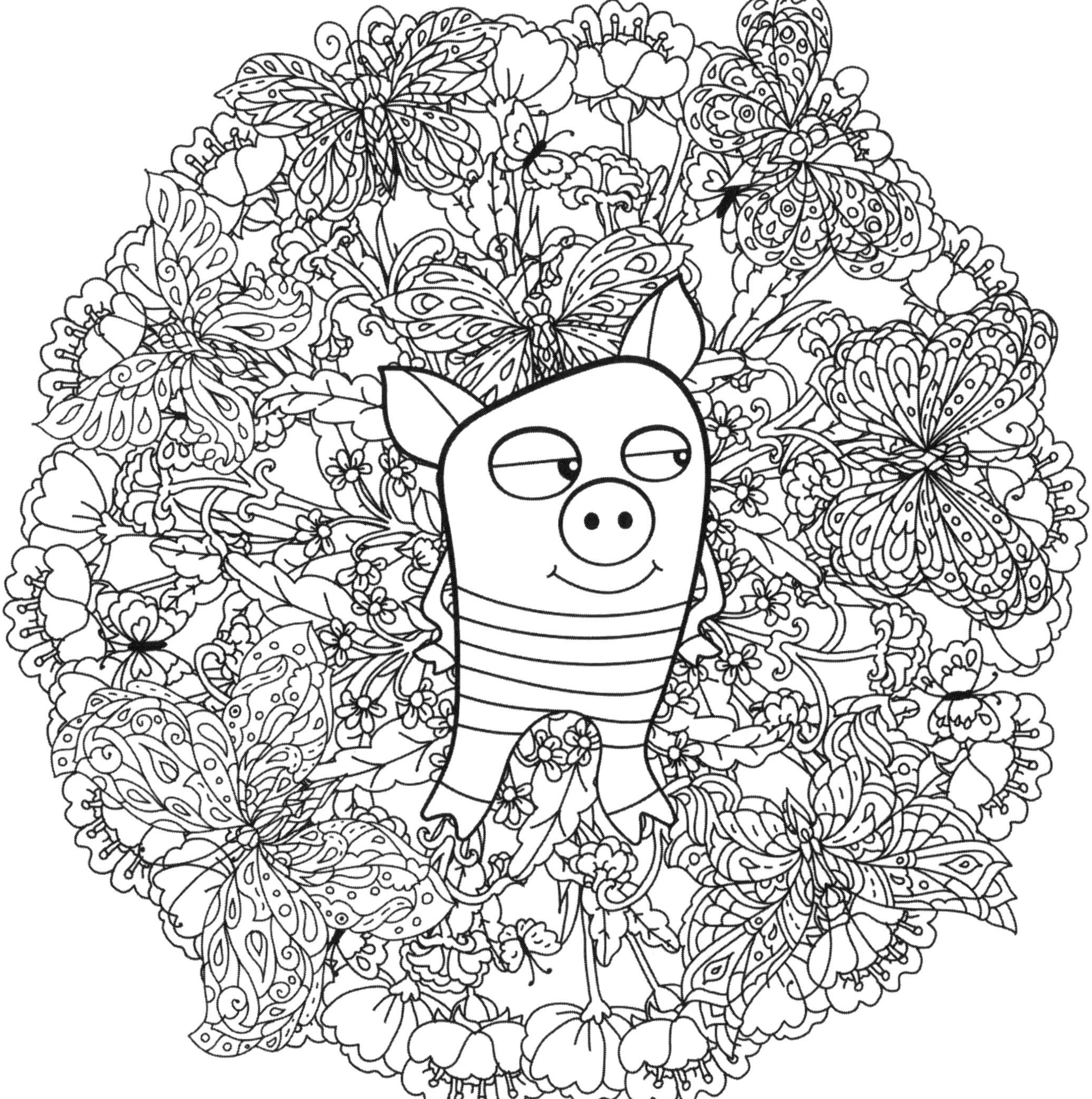

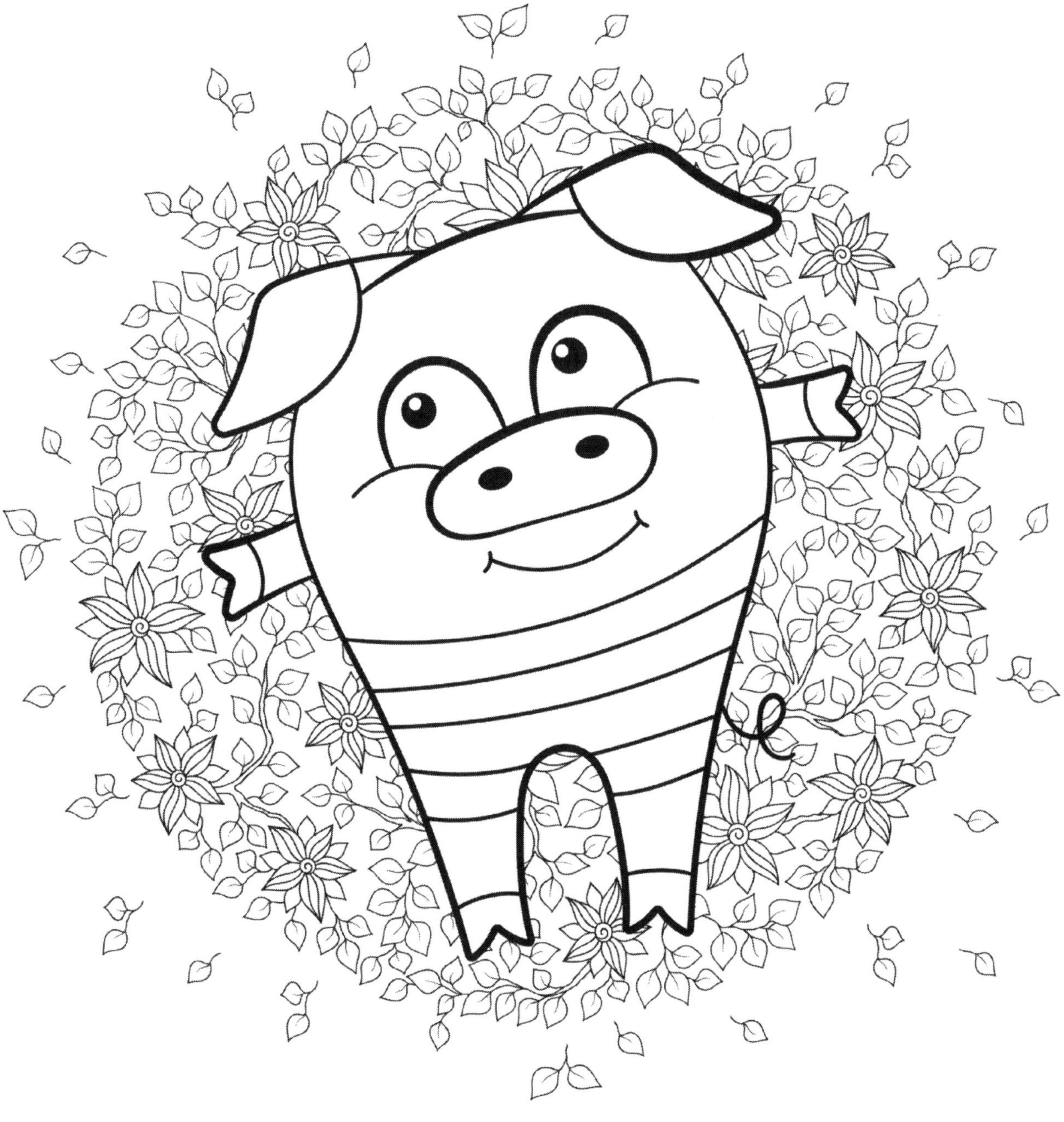

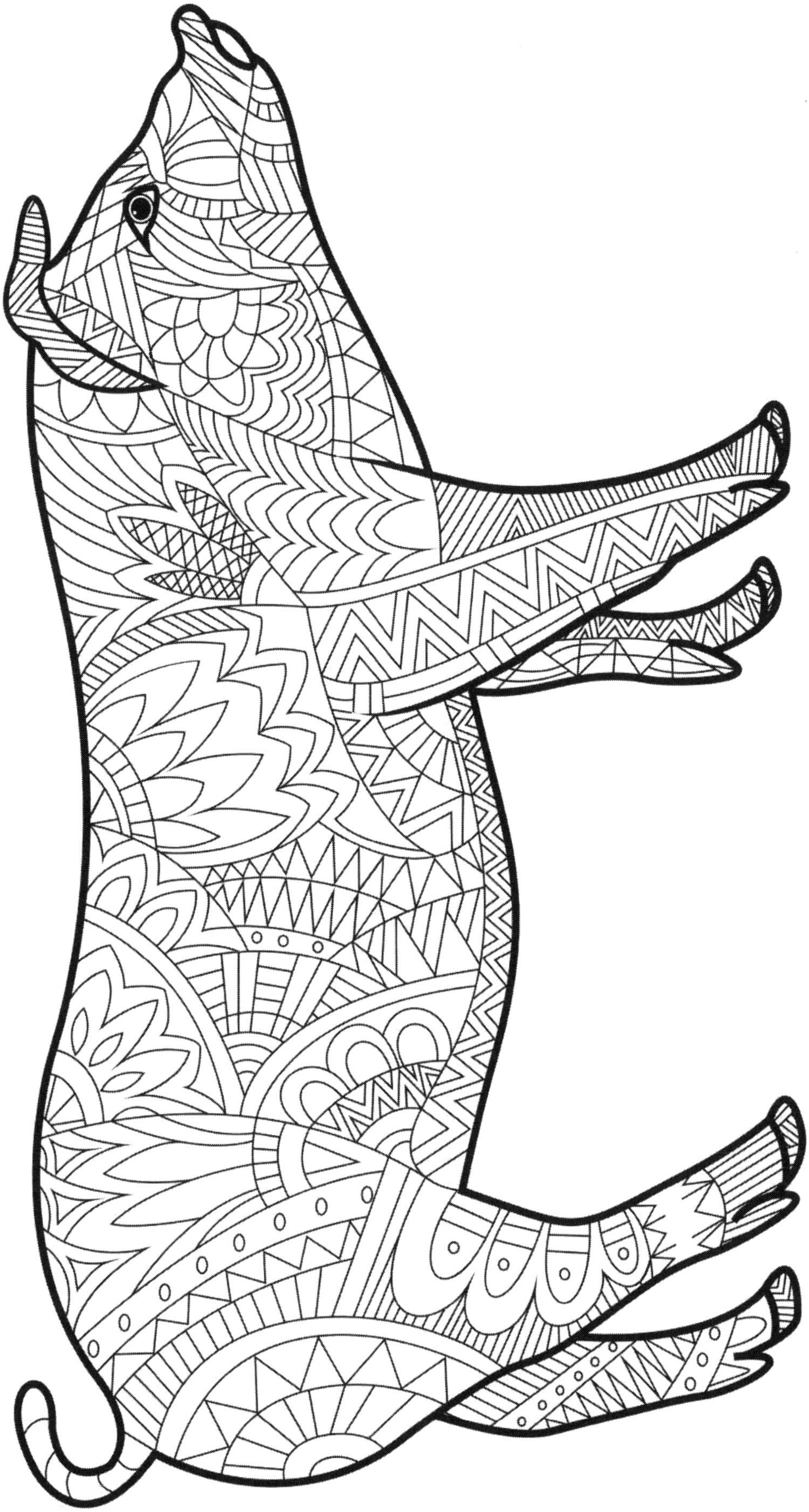

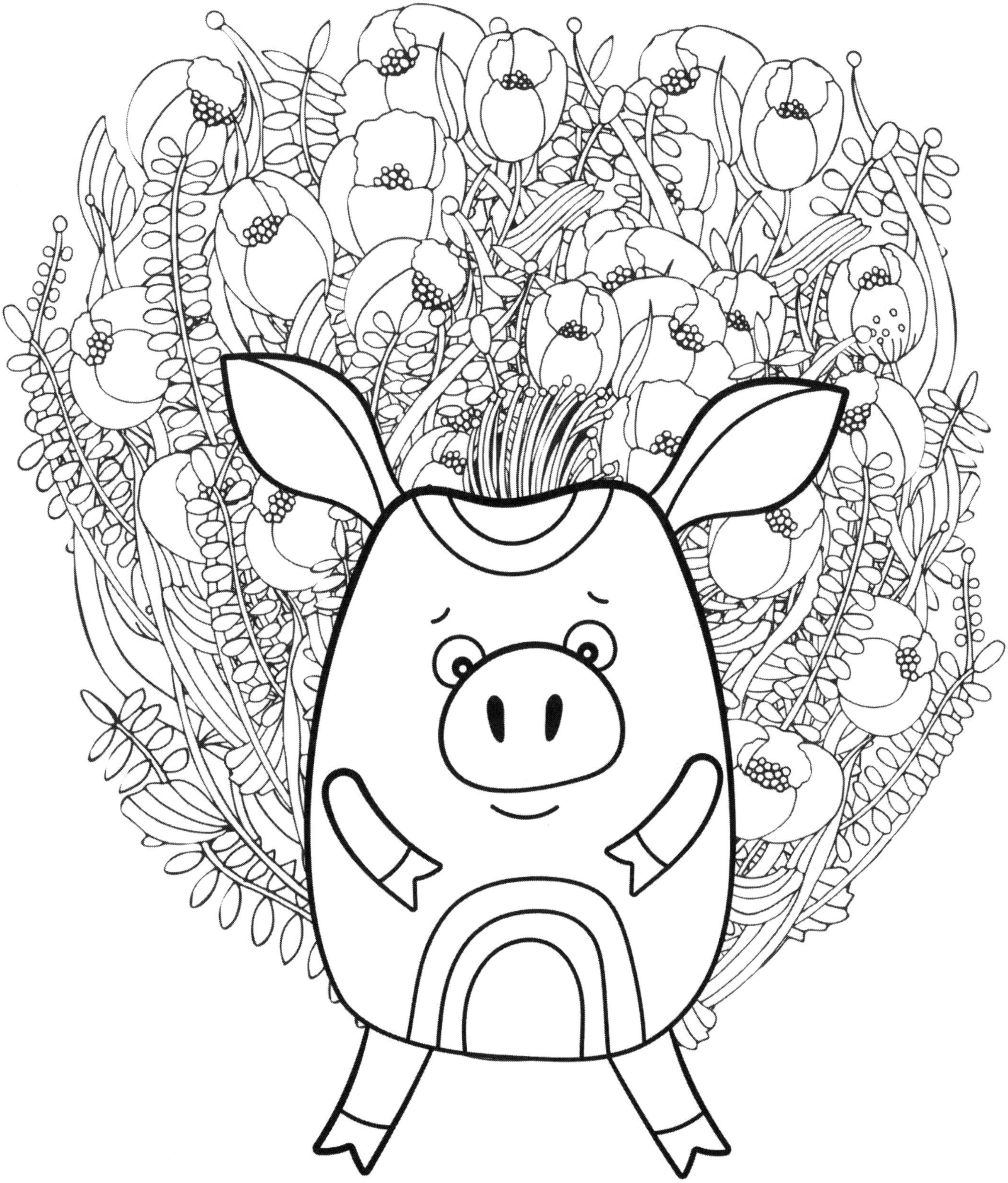

68832496R00031

Made in the USA
Lexington, KY
20 October 2017